I am
Jackie Robinson

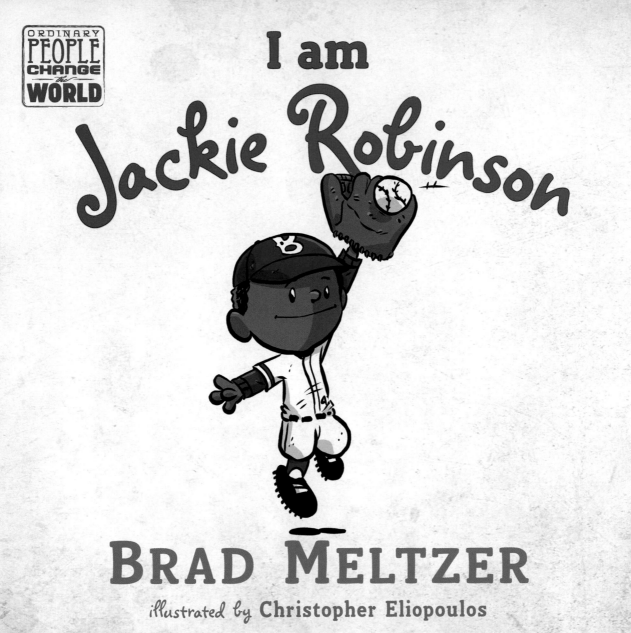

BRAD MELTZER

illustrated by Christopher Eliopoulos

DIAL BOOKS FOR YOUNG READERS an imprint of Penguin Group (USA) LLC

I am **Jackie Robinson.**

Sometimes it's hard to be brave.
My mother was brave. And she liked brave people.
When I was born, the youngest of five kids,
she even named me after someone brave.

But having a brave name doesn't make you a brave person.
In fact, as a kid, I didn't like sleeping alone.
I used to sleep in my mom's bed.
Even when she tried to bribe me, I wouldn't leave.

One of my scariest moments
came when I was eight years old.
I was outside and a girl
from across the street called
me a terrible name.

I was so mad, I yelled a name
right back at her.

Her father came running
immediately.

He didn't like it that a black
boy was standing up to his
white daughter.

We were the only black family
on our block.

I don't remember who
threw the first rock.

But the fight was on.
Me versus her dad.

GET 'IM, DAD.

I had a good arm. But no one wins in a rock fight.
Eventually, the girl's mother came out and broke it up.

Like I said, the world can be a scary place.
But even as a kid, there was one thing that always
made me happy . . .

Sports. And winning at sports.
(Okay, that's two things.)
I loved playing everything:
baseball, football, basketball,
soccer, marbles . . . even dodgeball.
All the kids would get in a circle.
White, black, Hispanic, Asian,
we all played together.
The rules were simple: If the ball
hit you, you were out.

I'd duck . . .

and of course
throw . . .

By the time I was done,
I'd be the last one standing.

ARE THEY MAD THAT I WON?

DUNNO.

FALL DOWN. MAYBE THEY WON'T NOTICE.

But the truth was . . .

jump . . .

leap . . .

and throw . . .

and throw.

They weren't mad at me for winning.
They appreciated the skill it took.
Those childhood games were some of the only times I wasn't
judged by the color of my skin.

Still, that didn't make all of my problems go away.

At the local public pool in Brookside Park, you could only go swimming if you were white.

If your skin was black, they locked you out.

When people complained, they gave us one day each week. Wednesday.

Every Wednesday, from 2 to 5 P.M., they'd open the pool to anybody black, Mexican, or Asian.

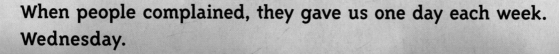

So how do you win when you feel like you're fighting the entire world?

My mother, who worked as a maid, showed me the answer.

Back then, we were so poor, we sometimes ate only two meals a day.

To help us out, every Saturday night the local bakery would let us take their leftovers.

And the milkman—back when milk was delivered to your house—would give us whatever extra he had.

We weren't the only ones struggling for money.

My mom took the extra food and shared it with all our neighbors.

That's how we got to be friends with everyone in the neighborhood.

It was one of my mom's best lessons: When you do something good, it brings out the good in others.

Plus, the more our neighbors got to know us, the more they realized just how much black and white people were alike.

I learned a similar lesson from a local mechanic named Carl Anderson.

He saw the group of boys I used to hang out with.

We called ourselves the Pepper Street gang.

We were a bunch of poor kids.

For fun, we'd throw dirt clods at cars, and swipe golf balls from the local course.

When he saw what we were doing, Mr. Anderson took me aside.
He didn't lose his temper.
Calm as could be, he told me . . .

What Mr. Anderson said that day, it got to me.
With the help of my pastor, I stopped hanging out with the gang.
From there, I threw myself even deeper into my favorite activity . . .

Sports. And winning at sports.
Especially baseball.

As a teenager, I could run so fast, a local reporter noticed that in nearly every game I stole second, third, and home at least once!

In college, I became the first UCLA student ever to letter in four sports in the same season:
Baseball . . .

and football . . .

and basketball . . .

and track.

But the same problems kept coming back.

When the college newspaper wrote a nice article about me, one of my own white teammates purposely smashed into my leg, trying to injure me. He was mad that the article said something nice about a black person.

By the time I got out of the army, it still didn't matter that I was one of the best athletes in the country. If you wanted to play professional sports, you had to be white.

Back then, if you were the world champs, it meant you were the *white* champs. In all of Major League Baseball, not a single team had even one black player.

Oh, and did I mention that if you were on a black team, the pay was worse, the food was worse, and sometimes, the only place to sleep was on the bus?

But that was all about to change . . .

Thanks to a man named Branch Rickey. Rickey was the president of the Brooklyn Dodgers, one of the most popular baseball teams ever.

I HAVE AN IDEA.

THE DODGERS WILL **SECRETLY**... LOOK AT BLACK PLAYERS.

With so many players fighting in World War II, Rickey had a plan for filling his team.

After searching all across the
United States and the world . . .

Branch Rickey found me.

I'M JACKIE ROBINSON.

NICE TO MEET YOU.

Mr. Rickey told me that he knew I was a good ballplayer. But he wanted to know whether I had the guts.

He warned me that many white people would be mad to see a black player.

On April 18, 1946, at 27 years old, I was given my shot. At Roosevelt Stadium in Jersey City, New Jersey, I played my first official game for the Montreal Royals, the Brooklyn Dodgers' farm team.

You better believe I was terrified. I didn't want to let people down. Then at 3:04 P.M., in my first at bat, I . . .

. . . was thrown out at first.

Thousands of black spectators had come to see what I could do. Thousands of white people were there too, convinced that a black player couldn't possibly be as good as a white one.

It was up to me to prove them wrong.

The next time I came up was in the third inning.
There were two men on base.
The pitcher decided on a fastball.

I can still see it coming, chest-high, down the middle.
But this time . . .

When the ball finally landed, 340 feet away in the left-field stands, no one could say that a black man can't play as well as a white man.

Some called it a home run.
Others called it *history*.

That afternoon, in five at bats, I hit and got on base four times.
I stole second twice.
And I scored four runs.

When the game was done, I couldn't get to the locker room because I was so mobbed by fans.

Black, white, young, old—even the folks rooting for the other team!—they were cheering.

For me.

Still, that didn't mean it was easy.

When I started playing for the Brooklyn Dodgers, lots of players didn't want me there.

Pitchers threw fastballs at my head.

Runners stepped on me with their cleats.

Catchers even spit on my shoes.

And they weren't just coming after me.

They told me that if I kept playing, they'd hurt my son.

Was I mad? Yes.

Was I scared? Yes.

But I never let it stop me.

KRAKK!

I TOLD YOU THE "B" IS FOR *BOOM!*

THE "B" IS FOR *BROOKLYN,* GENIUS.

Game after game, I kept playing . . . knowing I wasn't just playing for myself.

Each time, more and more people, black and white, were cheering.

In the stands, fans wore "I'm for Jackie" buttons.

And slowly, eventually . . .

We were all playing together. Black, white, Asian, Hispanic . . .
baseball opened up to everyone.
(It was just like those childhood games of dodgeball!)
    Through the simple game of baseball, the country saw
a new possibility.
    A new option.
    All they needed was for someone to go first.

In life, people tried to scare me.
They wanted to stop me.
They wanted to make me go away.
Why? Because I was different.

Each time, I wanted to fight back.
But for real change to come, you need
to lead by example.

Being a leader takes bravery.
But remember this: No one is born brave.
No matter how big or small you are,
there will always be things that scare you.
It's okay to be afraid.
Just don't let it stop you.

There is real power in each and every one of us.
Use that power to do what's right.
Use that power for a cause that you believe in.
And most of all, use that power to lead and help others.

I am Jackie Robinson.
I will always lead the way.
And I hope you will too.

When others see your example, they'll stand with you.
It's the only way the world ever gets changed:
Together.

"A life is not important except in the impact it has on other lives."
—JACKIE ROBINSON

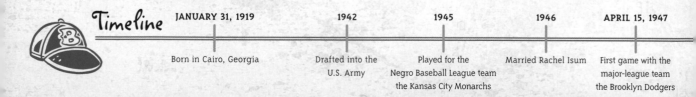

Timeline

JANUARY 31, 1919	1942	1945	1946	APRIL 15, 1947
Born in Cairo, Georgia	Drafted into the U.S. Army	Played for the Negro Baseball League team the Kansas City Monarchs	Married Rachel Isum	First game with the major-league team the Brooklyn Dodgers

Branch Rickey

Jackie, age 6 (second from left),
with his mother and siblings

Jackie playing
college football

Jackie at a college
track-and-field
event

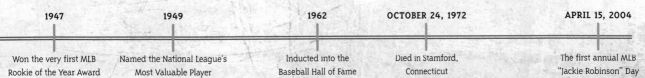

1947	1949	1962	OCTOBER 24, 1972	APRIL 15, 2004
Won the very first MLB Rookie of the Year Award	Named the National League's Most Valuable Player	Inducted into the Baseball Hall of Fame	Died in Stamford, Connecticut	The first annual MLB "Jackie Robinson" Day

Jonas, this book is for you. It's also for my Dad, your Pop.
Neither of you can be described without your
pure and passionate love of sports.
And Jonas, even when Pop couldn't walk,
he'd drive his car up to the fence,
just to watch you play baseball.
—B.M.

For my father-in-law, James Verde.
He cried the day I asked for his daughter's hand
and treated me like a son every day after.
And now we miss him every day.
—C.E.

Special thanks to Sharon Robinson for reading an early draft and making sure
we did justice to her father's story. We owe your whole family, Sharon.

SOURCES

I Never Had It Made: An Autobiography of Jackie Robinson by Jackie Robinson (Ecco, 2003)
Jackie Robinson: A Biography by Arnold Rampersad (Knopf, 1997)
Jackie Robinson: American Hero by Sharon Robinson (Scholastic, 2013)

FURTHER READING FOR KIDS

Who Was Jackie Robinson? by Gail Herman (Grosset & Dunlap, 2010)
Stealing Home by Robert Burleigh (Simon & Schuster, 2007)
Teammates by Peter Golenbock (HMH Books, 1992)

DIAL BOOKS FOR YOUNG READERS
An imprint of Penguin Random House LLC, New York

Text copyright © 2015 by Fourty-four Steps, Inc. • Illustrations copyright © 2015 by Christopher Eliopoulos
Visit us online at penguinrandomhouse.com

Library of Congress Cataloging-in-Publication Data
Meltzer, Brad.
I am Jackie Robinson / Brad Meltzer ; illustrated by Christopher Eliopoulos. • pages cm. — (Ordinary people change the world)
ISBN 978-0-8037-4086-0 (hardcover) • 1. Robinson, Jackie, 1919–1972—Juvenile literature. 2. Baseball players—United States—Biography—Juvenile literature. 3. African American baseball players—
Biography—Juvenile literature. 4. Discrimination in sports—United States—History—Juvenile literature. 5. Baseball—United States—History—Juvenile literature. I. Title.
GV865.R6M45 2015 796.357092—dc23 [B] 2014017473

Photo on page 38 by Bob Sandberg for *Look* magazine, 1954. Page 39: Branch Rickey photo © Bettmann/Corbis; family photo © Hulton Archive/Getty Images;
photo of Jackie playing football © Bettmann/Corbis; track-and-field photo by Maurice Terrell for *Look* magazine, 1945.

Manufactured in China on acid-free paper • 10 9 8 7
Designed by Jason Henry • Text set in Triplex • The artwork for this book was created digitally.